COUGAR

COUGAR

Kay McDearmon

Illustrated with photographs

DODD, MEAD, & COMPANY
New York

ACKNOWLEDGMENT

I am grateful to wildlife biologist Maurice G. Hornocker, Ph. D., who has studied the cougar extensively in its natural habitat, for acting as a consultant and for reviewing my manuscript for accuracy.

All photographs are courtesy of Fotowest.

Library of Congress Cataloging in Publication Data
McDearmon, Kay.
    Cougar.
    SUMMARY: Text and photographs follow a mother cougar as she teaches her cubs the ways of life in the wilderness.
    1. Pumas—Juvenile literature. [1. Pumas] I. Title.
QL737.C23M34   599′.74428   77–6086
ISBN 0–396–07468–5

To my sisters

INTRODUCTION

The cougar once had perhaps the widest distribution of any mammal in the Western Hemisphere. It ranged from the Atlantic to the Pacific oceans and from British Columbia to the tip of South America. And it lived—and still does—in such diverse areas as deserts, swamps, prairies, tropical jungles, and subalpine forests.

Because of its enormous original range, the cougar has acquired many names. Among them are mountain lion, catamount, and panther. The Inca Indians of Peru called the animal the puma. Whatever it is popularly called, its scientific name is *Felis concolor*, which means cat of the same color.

As the white man populated North America the cougar

gradually vanished from much of its range. The big cat now appears in areas where man rarely ventures. In the United States cougars are confined largely to rugged mountain areas in our western and southwestern states.

Experts estimate that as many as 6,500 may roam the western and southwestern United States. A few are reported hanging on in Florida's Everglades. The cougar population in Canada and Central and South America is unknown.

Over the years the cougar has been greatly misunderstood and relentlessly persecuted. Because it sometimes killed livestock, early settlers regarded the big cat as an enemy to be destroyed. Until recently, bounties were paid for each cougar killed. This system has taken a fearful toll. It is true that individual animals sometimes learn to kill domestic stock, but cougars generally pose little threat to the livestock industry.

Conservationists have been concerned about the cougar's effect upon the deer population. While this effect may differ from area to area, our research in the Idaho Primitive Area found that the big cats actually benefit the deer herds.

Cougars prey upon the weaker animals, thus helping to assure that the strongest survive. Also, after a kill, the herd moves to new feeding grounds. This reduces the chance of the remaining deer starving when food becomes scarce on the limited winter ranges.

Cougars have acquired a "bad" image in literature, movies, and television. This image is unjustified. The great cats kill only to eat, and they very rarely attack human beings. They are adaptive, intelligent, strong, and extremely agile—all qualities we admire in people.

Fortunately, our society is beginning to appreciate all wildlife more. And the cougar, long persecuted, is beginning to be recognized for what he is—a princely animal.

Maurice G. Hornocker, Ph. D.

Wildlife biologist,
U.S. Fish and Wildlife Service and
Idaho Cooperative Wildlife Research Unit,
University of Idaho, Moscow, Idaho

THE GOLDEN EAGLE was circling in the sky looking for a tasty meal when it saw a cougar cub on a rocky ledge. Tucking in its wings, it dived. Then, to brake its flight, the huge bird spread out its broad wings. It was about ready to snatch the little cougar with its sharp, curved claws when the cub looked up, saw the eagle, and quickly streaked off to his cave nearby.

It was a narrow escape. At most times his mother would have been around to protect her seven-pound cub. When he was this small she only left him and his twin sister when she was hungry, and even then she rarely traveled far.

That summer day her cubs had been asleep in their cave in Idaho's rugged wilderness when she had gone hunting.

11

Soon the male cub had awakened and wandered outside, exposing himself to danger.

Awhile before her cubs were born, their mother had roamed around her home range searching for a ready-made shelter for them. This cave under a ledge high on a cliff was ideal. Few black bears, coyotes, or foxes who might fancy one of her kittens for lunch would be likely to pass by, or if they did, to discover the well-hidden cave.

At their birth in June the spotted cubs each weighed only about one pound and were about twelve inches long, with tails ringed like a raccoon.

Blind at first, the furry babies had to fumble around the cave to find their mother's nipples. They could hear her purr as they drank her warm milk, but they couldn't see her for two weeks.

Those days the cubs did little more than nurse and cuddle up against their mother's soft, tawny fur and sleep. But soon they began to crawl, and act like cats—spitting, hissing, and growling at each other.

Now, at six weeks, they sometimes romped outside the cave while their strong, handsome, amber-eyed mother watched them. They tossed leaves and feathers around. They tumbled over fallen logs and sagebrush. They never tired of chasing each other. And they played with their mother's long tail.

When they wrestled, sometimes the toddlers bit and clawed at each other. Once the male bit his sister's ear so hard that she squealed with pain. Another time he reached for his mother's rump with his sharp teeth. She promptly cuffed him.

To nourish herself and to provide milk for her little ones, the cougar had to hunt. This she did mostly within her home range of about fifteen square miles. Like all cats, she could see extremely well in the dark, and she hunted almost as often during the night as during the day. She usually traveled around eight miles over rough country, looping back and forth, but she could cover as much as twenty-five miles in one night.

Deer was the cougar's favorite food. But even though the snow was almost melted on the slopes, finding deer was

Mule deer

not easy as the herds were scattered over the vast mountain terrain. And even when she saw, heard, or scented a big-eared, mule deer he was apt to escape before she could spring upon him.

Fawns had their own way of eluding the cougar. One day when she was climbing up a steep, grassy hillside a fawn was hiding in a nearby thicket. The cougar couldn't see the baby deer because his spotted fur blended with the surroundings. She couldn't hear him because he was lying quietly—not making the slightest sound. And because he lay so quietly, there was little chance the wind would blow any deer scent to her nostrils.

The cougar was not a fussy eater, and when she couldn't find big game such as deer or elk, she might catch a coyote,

Coyote

a bobcat, or even a skunk. She might also pounce upon a whistling marmot, a pocket gopher out for a rare stroll, or any other small animal that wandered near.

The cougar could go days without eating, and she often did. But her cubs soon needed meat if they were to build powerful muscles like their mother. After they were about two months old she hunted more, trying to satisfy both her needs and theirs.

As the cubs grew larger and stronger, they sometimes left their hideout while their mother hunted. Once when she was away longer than usual, her more timid female cub slipped out of the cave and tested the warm sunshine. As she ventured into the timber, a coyote saw her and gave chase.

The fleeing cub leaped over logs and zigzagged around trees. Then, with the coyote only a few feet behind her, she clambered up a pine tree. He couldn't climb, so the cub was safe there. But, instead of leaving, the coyote remained at the base of the tree, barking and howling. Finally, he gave up and wandered off. Only then did the frightened cub dare to jump down.

Meanwhile, her mother was having her troubles trying to catch deer. After three had eluded her, she spied an old doe nibbling grass in a meadow a short distance from the herd. At once the cougar lowered her head and crouched in the grass, creeping along noiselessly on her fur-padded feet. Her tawny fur blended with the terrain, making her hard to see. And each time the deer raised its head, the cougar halted until the doe started grazing again.

Once she came close, the cougar stayed under cover and waited, her steely eyes watching the doe as it drifted toward her. Suddenly, the cougar leaped onto her back and bit deep into the doe's neck with her long, sharp canine teeth. It was all over very quickly. The startled herd galloped off into the forest.

Long-tailed magpies waiting in the sky swooped down to join the cougar at her dinner. All they managed to get was a peck or two before the cougar chased them off.

She ate until her stomach bulged. Then she set aside chunks of the flesh to bring back to her cubs, and covered the carcass with a pile of dirt, twigs, and leaves. For about a week afterward the family feasted upon deer. But two weeks slipped by before the cougar caught another.

Until then, the cubs dined on the smaller prey their mother caught. As they ate a larger amount of meat, they nursed less and less, and finally not at all.

At first after their meals the cougar washed her cubs, licking their fur all over with her tongue. Little by little, the cubs learned to groom themselves.

Then all three would take a nap. As they awakened,

they yawned and stretched, arching their backs like house cats. Sometimes they were asleep again a few minutes later.

One day, after one of their long naps, the cougar led her little family out of their snug birth cave. The three-month-old cubs didn't know it, but they would not return to it again.

As they followed their mother along mountain trails in her home range, the curious cubs investigated everything. They sniffed at plants and turned over pine cones. They wandered into rock caves and into caverns made by fallen pine or fir trees. And they jumped over fallen logs.

The cougar still was the lone hunter in her family. But before she went on a foray, she left her cubs in dense brush, high grass, or in a cave or den to conceal them while she was away. These days when she returned, she led her cubs to whatever prey she had caught.

After their dinner one night their mother looked around and saw a huge cougar coming down the steep canyon slope. The animal was seven feet long—from the tip of its nose to the tip of its tail—and weighed more than 150 pounds. Such a hefty cougar had to be a male.

He could have been the cubs' father, but in any case their mother no longer had any interest in him. She had stayed with him only about two weeks after they had mated in the spring, and he had then returned to his own home range. He or any other full-grown cougar might attack her cubs. So she quickly led them off into the trees and hid them in a thicket until the male passed.

A few days later when the cougar was hunting, she saw a flock of bighorn sheep busily feeding upon a grassy slope. One sheep was standing upon a boulder acting as a lookout.

Head down and belly low, the cougar inched her way in the grass toward the sheep. She carefully set her hind feet down in the tracks of her forefeet. That way there was less chance that she would snap a twig or dislodge a rock and so alert the sentry. And, as it happened, she was moving upwind so the wind was carrying her scent behind her and away from the grazing sheep.

Suddenly, the wind changed direction. The sheep guarding the flock caught the cougar's scent and scampered up the slope. The other sheep swiftly followed.

The cougar bounded after a ram in the rear of the disappearing flock. She could climb almost anywhere a bighorn could, using her long tail for balance, and she was a speedy sprinter. But she couldn't keep up her fast pace in a long chase, especially up a steep, rocky slope. So this time she had to give up.

Bighorn sheep

But whenever she was hungry and she could find deer, she stalked them. She didn't hide in a tree and wait for one to wander by and then leap upon it. In this vast wilderness she could starve before any prey at all passed by.

While hunting at dusk once that summer the cougar saw a lone buck rubbing his new antlers against a pine tree to scrape off the velvet and to polish them. This time the cougar stayed under cover, unseen, unheard, and un-scented by the busy deer until she was close enough to pounce upon him. Then suddenly she leaped upon his back and broke his neck.

Even if the cougar had completely covered the carcass after the family's supper, any other meat-eating animal prowling in the area could have scented it. Now, as she had left an antler exposed, it could also be seen easily.

A bushy-tailed red fox hunting for a quick meal the next morning saw the antler rising above the ground. Once on the scene, he looked around, sniffed the air, and listened. Then he hurriedly brushed off some of the dirt and leaves from the carcass, and ripped into the meat.

Red fox

When he heard the big cat and her cubs stirring in the dense brush, he bolted into the timber before the awakening cougar could catch his scent or see him. There he hid behind a log so he could slip back later to finish his dinner when the cougars fell asleep again.

Badger

One August day before they had finished eating the deer, the cougar awoke from a nap to see a badger digging nearby. He is a fierce fighter, but as his rear was toward the cougar, she could easily have captured him, but she didn't even try. She killed only when she was hungry and never caught more prey than her little family could consume.

Soon colder, shorter days signaled a new season. With fall, pine cones ripened and scattered their seeds. Squirrels scooped up the seeds and nuts on the ground and stored them in their holes for the winter. Bears gorged themselves on berries to fatten themselves before sleeping away much

Bear

of the winter in their dens. And before long golden eagles and red-tailed hawks began winging their way to lower elevations for the winter.

Meanwhile, at the higher levels icy winds howled through the mountains and snow blanketed much of the cougars' home range. As the snow piled up in the meadows and upon their favorite slopes, the deer and elk could no longer reach the grass—a vital part of their vegetarian diet.

After a fierce snowstorm in November an old cow elk led her herd down from the high country. The other elk herds all followed, straggling along trails they had used in other years to their winter feeding grounds at lower elevations. The deer, too, moved to this area where winters, while still severe, were less so and snow wasn't nearly so deep.

The cougar could remain and limit her hunting to her summer range. But with the deer and the elk gone and most rodents hibernating for the winter, she would surely starve. So she and her family also wandered to the lower levels.

Along the way the cougar often stopped at the base of a fir tree, and raked her claws along the trunk of the tree to sharpen them. Her cubs also sharpened their claws, sometimes on fallen logs or stumps.

One day a blizzard burst over the land. The cougars' new darker and heavier winter coats protected them against cold, wintry weather. But with snow blowing and drifting they could hardly see or move. They sought shelter under a cluster of fir trees, and stayed there for two days until the storm finally ended.

Another day when snow suddenly swirled all around them, the cougar stopped at the entrance to a den. When she peered inside she saw a big black bear curled up in a corner, asleep. Quietly, she backed out of the den. If she had awakened the bear, he might have rushed at her or attacked one of her cubs.

Luckily, in this primitive land, shelters were not hard to find. Soon the cougars wandered into a cave recently deserted by a pack rat. Lying around were old dry bones, sticks, feathers, leaves, and even a stolen camper's watch. These assorted playthings kept the cubs amused while the storm lasted.

By the time the cougar reached her winter range in the Salmon River Mountains the cubs were about six months old. The male cub now weighed forty pounds, five more than his sister.

Snowshoe hares sometimes hopped into the cougar's new world. She caught one now and then, but in their white winter coats it was hard for her to see them on a snowy day. And because the hair on their feet acted like snowshoes the hares could skim across even deep snow, while it slowed down the 100-pound cougar.

The cougar's stalk-and-leap style sometimes made hunting deer and elk in the snow harder, too. But on their winter range the herds were less scattered than they were in the high country. With more chances to catch them, the cougar brought more down.

Most animals hunt only prey smaller than they are, so it is truly remarkable that the cougar would try to capture deer or elk at all. But to survive in this Idaho wilderness she must catch them.

A full-grown deer can be two or three times heavier than

Elk

the cougar, and an elk can be up to ten times heavier. They have fearful weapons. One lash of their hoofs, or a well-placed jab from the sharp antlers of a male, can seriously wound or kill. To avoid this danger the cougar sprang from the rear and usually stalked young, old, or under-nourished animals rather than mature, healthy ones.

One February day when she was hunting, the cougar saw elk tracks in the snow. After following them for a few miles up a steep hillside she saw a herd of elk. Some were digging through the light snow to get at the grass below, some were browsing on aspen twigs, and some were eating the stems of bitterbrush.

For her target the cougar chose a thin, old male that was unknowingly limping toward her. She stalked him slowly, hugging the ground as usual. Then she hid behind a fallen log and waited until the elk reached for a twig about fifteen feet away from her. One leap and the cougar was upon his back and at his neck. The bull jerked his head, but couldn't throw the cougar off or escape. A few minutes and his struggle was over.

The elk lay close to the trail, and there it would be easy for another animal to find. The cougar couldn't drag an elk or deer *up* a slope. But the powerful cougar dragged this elk weighing 800 pounds down the slope before eating her fill and hiding the remains under a willow tree. Then she and her family feasted upon it for several days.

With warmer spring days the piled-up snow began

melting, and tender, new shoots of grass began appearing. High in the sky above the canyon glossy black ravens courted. Steelhead trout swam from the sea up rivers to spawn in the mountain streams. And on the grassy slopes buck deer that had shed their antlers during the winter began growing new ones.

There were times that spring when the cougar, usually the hunter, became the hunted. Once, as she was about to leave her cubs in a rocky crevice, she sniffed the air and caught a scent that she knew meant danger.

She also heard dogs barking in the distance. The cougar could easily dispatch a single dog, but a pack of barking dogs terrified her. She quickly whistled an alarm to her cubs and bounded up over the ridge, plunging down and into an icy creek with her cubs close behind.

The yelping dogs pursued the cougars into the water, but then they lost their tracks. The dogs were still nosing around the ground searching for the tracks when the hunters caught up with the dogs and set them chasing the cougars again.

But by then the cougars had scaled a rocky bluff. There they were safe, as neither the dogs nor the hunters could follow them over the bare, jagged rocks.

The cougar's hunting that spring was quite successful. She caught several deer and an occasional elk for herself and her hungry cubs. But in mid-May these large prey were harder and harder to find, as both the deer and elk had started drifting back to their summer range. So the cougar and her cubs also wandered north to theirs.

Once in a canyon the cougar and her cubs came across

a miner's cabin, now almost in ruins. Inside, the cubs played with empty barrels, boxes, and tin cans, rolling them around. Then they nosed about outside.

Their mother waited quietly and patiently inside. She knew there might be a mouse or perhaps a pack rat in the walls or under the floor. Finally, a mouse came out of hiding and skittered across the uneven wooden planks. The big cat sprinted after him and pounced upon him. This snack was too small to share with her cubs.

Soon after, the cougar hunted for a meal she could share with her young ones. Standing near the top of a cliff she saw a woolly white mountain goat. He would do nicely.

Now and then she had caught a mountain goat, and she had never spurned chasing her prey over steep, rocky slopes. But this time her skill wasn't tested. Just as she began climbing, a huge rock bounded down the slope, alerting the goat, and he trotted off.

The cougar had been hunting for two days when she saw a porcupine chewing bark off a pine tree. She scrambled up the trunk, crept out onto the limb supporting him, and shoved him to the ground. Then she jumped down after him. She circled around the slow-moving rodent, suddenly dashing in, pouncing upon him and crushing him in her powerful jaws.

Along with his flesh she and her cubs ate some of the porcupine's quills. For them this was no hazard, as the quills would dissolve in their digestive tracts.

A few days later the cougar and her cubs reached their summer range. Shortly after, the cubs had their first birthday. By then their fur had lost almost all of its markings. The male cub weighed seventy-five pounds, his smaller sister, sixty. Both of them were developing powerful muscles like their mother.

Early that summer the cougar began teaching her yearlings to hunt. Sometimes she took her male cub with her; sometimes she took his sister. Separately they had a chance to observe her hunting skill. She caught a raccoon busy eating huckleberries. She captured a beaver sunning himself on a creek bank. And she stalked several deer and a few elk. She rarely missed, once she leaped upon one.

By the time they returned to their winter range, the cubs had tried their new hunting skills many times. But almost all the animals they tried to catch escaped. Sometimes the cub wasn't quiet enough; sometimes it bounded from cover too soon; and sometimes it leaped too far. One time the male cub landed upon an old deer's back and promptly fell off. And many times the wind gave their presence away.

Once that winter, after the family had gone without food for several days, the cougar went hunting by herself. As she loped through the snow, two barking dogs began chasing her. She sprinted ahead for awhile, but soon the noisy dogs started closing the gap. Finally, when they were only a few feet behind her, the cougar clambered up a pine tree. There she snarled at them from a limb eighteen feet from the ground.

The hounds were baying excitedly at the base of the tree when two men appeared. For a few moments they were within striking distance of the cougar. She could easily have sprung from her perch in the tree and attacked them, but she remained on the limb.

This time the men were scientists, not hunters. So, instead of aiming a rifle at the cougar, one of the men fired a dart filled with a tranquilizing drug into her rump.

In a few minutes the drug made the cougar groggy. Then one of the men climbed up the tree and roped her foot, throwing one end of the rope over a limb. Then he carefully lowered her to the ground.

Once the cougar was there the men measured her, weighed her, and examined her. They marked her with numbered ear tags and tattooed the number on her body. The radio collar they slipped around her neck had a tiny transmitter inside to help them track her movements and learn more about her habits.

Later, on a bone-chilling February morning the cougar escaped rather than attack these men. One of them had just lifted himself up onto a narrow, rocky ledge to see where

the cougar had gone. There, to his surprise, he saw her standing on the far edge. She had only two choices: she could jump off the cliff, or move toward him. Without hesitating, she crouched and leaped, sailing over his head and landing beyond him.

These wintry days the cougar and her cubs were still together. Then, one blustery March day when her cubs were about twenty months old, their mother left them.

Just as the little family was finishing its meal of venison, she walked off and started down the hillside. She didn't look back at all, and somehow the cubs seemed to know that she wouldn't return.

Where was she going? She knew from earlier wanderings that there was more prey and cover in the next territory held by an old male cougar. So she might see if he had left or died. If either had happened, she would take over his old home.

But first, after leaving her cubs, the cougar searched for a new mate. She soon met a male from a nearby territory, and about three months later she had three new babies. She would have another litter about every two years. And she could live another ten years in the wild.

The two young cougars she left behind traveled together for awhile. One day they separated to hunt, the male cougar dropping into the canyon, the female exploring around the ridge. Some time later, they called each other with birdlike whistles and came together to continue their hunting.

Between them the cubs caught a nesting blue grouse, a whistling marmot, a beaver sitting on a creek bank combing his fur with his toenails, and a porcupine chewing antlers shed by a buck deer. The male cub was the more skillful hunter, but as yet each deer he tried to stalk escaped before he could bound from cover.

He deserted his sister after about two weeks to search for a territory that he could call his own. While traveling he often saw scrapes—scented mounds of leaves, dirt, and pine or fir needles. When he sniffed these piles he knew he was in another cougar's home range. Finally, after roaming around the mountains for almost a year, he found a vacant area of about twenty-five square miles with enough prey and cover to please him.

Meanwhile, his sister also scouted around the rugged mountains hunting for a smaller home range for herself. Many months later, when she found one, she set out to find a mate.

Altogether, the two young cougars had survived the most dangerous times of their lives. While they were little, if their mother hadn't caught enough prey, they could have starved. When she was away hunting, any predator that found their hideaway might have eaten them.

Once on their own, the cubs faced similar threats. While

they practiced their hunting skills they could starve. And
without their mother to protect them, alert them to danger,
and lead them to safety, they were more likely to become
the victims of hunters—animal or human.

Yet, as mature cougars with powerful muscles, they
were fast becoming "the athletes of the wild." With luck,
these intelligent, handsome animals with soft, tawny fur
and lovely amber eyes would grace their mountain wilderness for years to come.